R

Great Strides

Critical Thinking Skills

Rigby®
A Harcourt Achieve Imprint

www.Rigby.com
1-800-531-5015

ACKNOWLEDGMENTS

STAFF CREDITS

Editorial: Vicky Aeschbacher, Heera Kang, Lori Najar, Tina Posner
Design: Amy Braden, Joan Cunningham, Joyce Spicer

ILLUSTRATIONS

P. 30 Ken Gamage; p. 36 Jason Abbott; p. 42 Sean Tiffany; p. 46 Marty Baumann

PHOTOGRAPHY

P. 14 ©AP Photo/Julie Jacobson; p. 15 ©Jeff Cadge/Getty Images; p. 20 ©AP Photo/Anja Niedringhaus; p. 21 ©Leonhard Foeger/Reuters/CORBIS; p. 27 ©Bettmann/CORBIS; p. 52 ©Mario Tama/Getty Images News; p. 53 ©Roger Ressmeyer/CORBIS; p. 58 ©Jesse D. Garrabrant/NBAE via Getty Images; p. 59 ©Catherine Steenkeste/NBAE via Getty Images.

Additional photography by Comstock Royalty Free, Photos.com Royalty Free and PhotoDisc/Getty Images.

YOUNG ADULT WRITERS

P. 30 Dana Davidson; p. 36 Alden Carter; p. 42 JoAnn Hernandez

ISBN 1-4189-2918-2

Printed in the United States of America

1 2 3 4 5 6 7 8 9 059 10 09 08 07 06 05

Critical Thinking Skills help you to make decisions about what you read.

So you will be able to:

- think about what the author says and decide if you agree.
- question whether the author is fair or biased.
- decide what's important to remember and use what you learn when reading more about that topic.

Table of Contents

HYPO
TELE KOM AUS TRIA
MIZUNO

Lesson 1

Critical Thinking Skills Roleplay

Student 1: The question asks us how the person who wrote this poem would feel about today's popular TV shows.

Student 2: They're really popular. It seems like everyone wants to be famous now.

Student 3: Well, it looks like the person who wrote this poem wasn't too interested in fame.

Student 1: Yeah, but her biography says that she turned out to be a really famous person.

Student 2: That happened after she died. She didn't try to be famous.

Student 3: Anyway, her poem says that it would be dreary. That means dull and depressing. So she's against fame.

Teacher: That's good thinking. See if you can figure out why she has this opinion of fame. That will help you answer the question.

Student 1: Well, she compares a famous person to a frog. I once saw a bullfrog all puffed up and looking very silly.

Student 2: Also, in the poem, the frogs are telling their names to an admiring bog. A bog is like a swamp.

Student 3: So to her, those people on TV might as well be frogs trying to get attention from a swamp. In other words, she'd probably think they were boring and silly for caring so much about fame.

Teacher: When you read, think about what the writer says and how the writer says it. That helps you understand the writer's viewpoint. Then decide if you agree. That's using critical thinking skills.

Your Turn

Read the list of tasks. Then sort them into the chart below. Remember, when you use critical thinking skills, you think about the reading in a more general way.

- Summarizing an article
- Listing events in the right order
- Deciding why the author wrote something
- Using story clues to predict what will happen next
- Deciding if school uniforms are a good idea
- Finding information on a chart or map

Critical Thinking Skills Are Good For	Critical Thinking Skills Are NOT Good For

Write Back...

The next time you need to make decisions about the information that you're reading, what will you do?

Separate Classrooms for BOYS AND GIRLS

Comprehension Skills

- **Lesson 2:** Recognizing Facts and Opinions
- **Lesson 3:** Assessing Evidence for Opinions

Reading Strategy

Use Background Knowledge
Use what you already know to help you understand what you read.

Boys and girls learn differently.

Look around your classroom. Do you see boys and girls? How would things change if your classmates were all boys or all girls? Would you be more comfortable? Experts say boys and girls learn differently. If boys and girls study in **separate** classrooms they will learn much faster.

All-Boy Classrooms

Boys are better learners if they go to school with other boys. Here's why. Boys are active learners. They often like to move around and make noise when they learn. They also learn better when they can compete with each other. They pay more attention and stay more interested.

Boys are more active learners.

Girls in all-girl classrooms do better in math, science, and computers.

All-Girl Classrooms

Girls **benefit** from all-girls classes, too. Girls work well in groups. They like to work together on projects. Most girls don't like to compete. When they are in classes with boys, sometimes girls appear to be quiet and shy. That's because they don't want to compete. In all-girl classrooms, girls can be themselves.

Why Not?

Some parents worry that their children will feel **isolated**. After all, in the real world boys and girls mix all the time. Some people think that boys in all-boys classes will not be able to deal with girls. Or girls will not understand boys. That's silly. Kids have lots of time on the playground, in clubs, and at home to get to know each other.

Of course, all-boy or all-girl classes are not better for everyone. Some girls like to compete and be active. Some boys like to work in groups. Still, most kids do better in separate classes. And shouldn't schools do what is best for most students? ■

What Do You Think?

Should girls and boys go to separate classes?

- ☐ Yes, they will learn in their own styles.
- ☐ No, they will not have a chance to get to know each other.

Vocabulary

separate: kept apart
benefit: gain from
isolated: alone or cut off from others

Lesson 2

Recognizing Facts and Opinions

Your Turn

Read "Separate Classrooms for Boys and Girls" again. Draw a line under facts and circle opinions. Then, write them into the chart below.

Facts (statements you can prove)	Opinions (feelings and beliefs)

Your Choice

Circle the correct answer.

1. **The reading says that the greatest benefit of all-boys schools is that boys —**

   A. stay interested in school.
   B. discover new subjects.
   C. enjoy reading.
   D. are more polite.

2. **Which is an opinion?**

   A. Boys learn differently than girls.
   B. Experts say boys are active learners.
   C. Separate classrooms are better for everyone.
   D. Most classrooms have both boys and girls.

3. **Which is a fact?**

   A. All girls like math and science.
   B. Most kids love school.
   C. Most classrooms have both boys and girls.
   D. All boys are loud.

4. **If someone is isolated she or he could be —**

   A. riding on a crowded bus.
   B. in an empty room.
   C. on a team playing baseball.
   D. running with friends.

(See answers for Critical Thinking Skills, Lesson 2 to check your work.)

Number Correct:

Write Back...

When are facts important as you read?

Lesson 3

Assessing Evidence for Opinions

Your Turn

Read the opinion in the top box. Reread the passage and circle three reasons the writer has this opinion. Then, draw a line under evidence for the opinion. Fill in the the chart with reasons and evidence. One has been done for you.

Opinion

All-boy and all-girl classrooms are the best way for kids to learn.

Reasons		
Girls are not as shy.		

Evidence		
They raise their hands and speak up in class.		

Your Choice

Circle the correct answer.

1 What does the writer of the passage think about all-boy and all-girl classes?

A. Schools need to keep boys and girls together.
B. It is a good idea for students.
C. It is not going to work in the future.
D. It can cause many new problems.

2 What evidence does the writer give for the opinion, "Boys are better learners if they go to school with other boys"?

A. Boys don't move around much when they learn.
B. Boys like "hard" classes.
C. Teachers like loud classes.
D. Boys like to be active when they learn.

3 Good evidence —

A. supports reasons.
B. is always interesting.
C. tells why a person believes something.
D. expresses an opinion.

4 What is meant by "Girls benefit from all-girls classes"?

A. Girls like all-girl classes.
B. Girls don't get along in all-girl classes.
C. Girls gain something from all-girl classes.
D. Girls are interested in all-girl classes.

(See answers for Critical Thinking Skills, Lesson 3 to check your work.)

Number Correct:

Write Back...

How do reasons and facts help people accept an opinion?

SURFING from WATER to LAND

An ocean thrill becomes a wild city ride.

Comprehension Skills

- **Lesson 4:** Making Generalizations
- **Lesson 5:** Connecting Across Texts

Reading Strategy

Stop and Think About What You Read

Often, readers rush through important details. Take a break as you read to make sure that you understand everything.

British sailors could not believe what they saw. People were standing on tall waves. The water curl carried them all the way to the beach. It was 1779 in Hawaii. The sailors were watching surfers—the first surfers they had ever seen.

Many sports change over time. The first surfers used small belly boards. Later, they stood up on boards twenty-four feet long.

In the 1950s, surfing became a national **craze**. From the beaches of Southern California came a new kind of music, fashion, and even movies. When people could not surf, they turned instead to homemade scooters. They **designed** these by nailing roller-skates to boxes. Then someone took away the box. They just stood on a board with wheels.

In the 1970s in Los Angeles, people began skateboarding in empty swimming pools. They bent down low. They did smooth twists and spins. It gave them the feeling of surfing on land. ■

Bethany Hamilton signs a surfboard. Bethany became famouse when she refused to give up surfing after a shark attack.

During the 1970s in Los Angeles it rarely rained. Swimming pools were left dry—perfect for skateboards!

Surfing Sea or Street

Wind in my face
Tells me my speed
Toes at the edge
Inching toward
A place of balance
Like a bird hopping
Onto a very thin branch
Then a downhill swoop
Leaning into the turns
And then up, catching air
Free falling fast
Bending at the knees
Taking the bumps
That come with landing
And ending
On a neat
Turn.

Vocabulary

craze: a popular trend or fad
designed: make

Lesson 4

Making Generalizations

Your Turn

Go back and circle two ideas that are alike. Underline other ideas that are alike. Use what you've marked to fill out the chart below.

Topic

Some examples say

Other examples say

Generalization

(A general idea that might be true in a lot of cases.)

Your Choice

Circle the correct answer.

1. **In 1779 British sailors came to Hawaii. What did they see?**
   - A. people fishing
   - B. people surfing
   - C. people skateboarding
   - D. people swimming

2. **Which generalization best matches this article?**
   - A. California is the only place people surf.
   - B. Surfing and skating are very different.
   - C. Surfing is hard to learn.
   - D. Surfing led to skateboarding.

3. **How are surfing and skateboarding related?**
   - A. Riders get the same kind of feeling.
   - B. They both started in the 1700s.
   - C. Both need an ocean.
   - D. They are not related.

4. **How did riders design homemade scooters?**
   - A. They rode low and smooth.
   - B. They put different parts together.
   - C. They used smaller surfboards.
   - D. They jumped curbs and ramps.

(See answers for Critical Thinking Skills, Lesson 4 to check your work.)

Number Correct:

Write Back...

How does it help you to make general statements about what you read?

Lesson 5

Connecting Across Texts

Your Turn

Go back and put a check mark next to details and ideas that both texts share. Write those in the space at the center of the chart. Write details that make each text special into the boxes with the text titles.

Surfing from Water to Land

Details Both Texts Share

Surfing Sea or Street

Your Choice

Circle the correct answer.

1. **What was the first skateboard made from?**

   A. a motorcycle
   B. a surfboard
   C. an ollie
   D. a scooter

2. **How can you tell what these texts are about?**

   A. from their titles and details
   B. from the list of skills
   C. from the dates and signal words
   D. from the vocabulary words and definitions

3. **What information do these texts have in common?**

   A. They both give a history of surfing.
   B. They help you understand the fun of surfing and skateboarding.
   C. They compare the dangers of surfing to skateboarding.
   D. They give instructions on how to build a skateboard.

4. **An example of another craze might be —**

   A. reading.
   B. book bags.
   C. school lunches.
   D. video games.

(See answers for Critical Thinking Skills, Lesson 5 to check your work.)

Number Correct:

Write Back...

How did thinking about the ideas in two texts help you?

Super Skier

Meet a great skier!

Comprehension Skills

- **Lesson 6:** Recognizing Bias and Viewpoint
- **Lesson 7:** Identifying an Author's Purpose

Reading Strategy

Question Yourself

As you read, ask yourself what the author is trying to do. Is he or she trying to convince you of something? How do you feel about what the author is trying to do?

Janica was born with the heart of a champion. She started skiing when she was just three years old. At first she was not very good. "She fell all the time," her father said. "We thought she would never learn." Janica was **determined** to become a skier, though. She practiced hard. Soon she learned to ski and became a great skier!

Janica and her brother loved to ski. They entered many races. The family traveled all over to watch them race. They did not have money to stay in hotels, so they had to camp out. Sometimes they slept in their car. Nothing could stop Janica from competing, though.

When Janica was 14, she entered twenty-two races. She won all of them! Two years later, Janica went to Japan for the Olympics. She finished in eighth place. That didn't stop her. Janica kept skiing.

Winning three gold medals would make anyone smile.

Janika needed strong knees to be a champion skier.

Janica skied so much that she hurt her knees. Her doctors told her that she should stop skiing. It was dangerous to keep skiing on her weak knees. Most people would stop skiing in a situation like that. Not Janica. She had three operations. The doctors helped her build her strength. Janica would not give in to her bad knees. She trained even harder. Soon she could race again. Janica was **invincible**!

Janica skied in the Olympics again. It was 2002. The Olympics were in the United States. Janica won three gold medals! They were the first gold medals for her country, Croatia. She became a hero in Croatia and around the world.

Janica is a brave athlete. She has won many races. **Poverty**, pain, and danger all tried to beat her. No way! This champion would not give up. ■

Vocabulary

determined: showing strength in purpose
invincible: cannot be beat
poverty: state of being poor

Lesson 6 Recognizing Bias and Viewpoint

Your Turn

Read "Super Skier" again. Circle any sentences or words that show you how the writer feels about Janica. Then, fill in the graphic organizer with good and bad things the writer says about Janica. You can tell the author's bias by which side of the graphic organizer has more evidence.

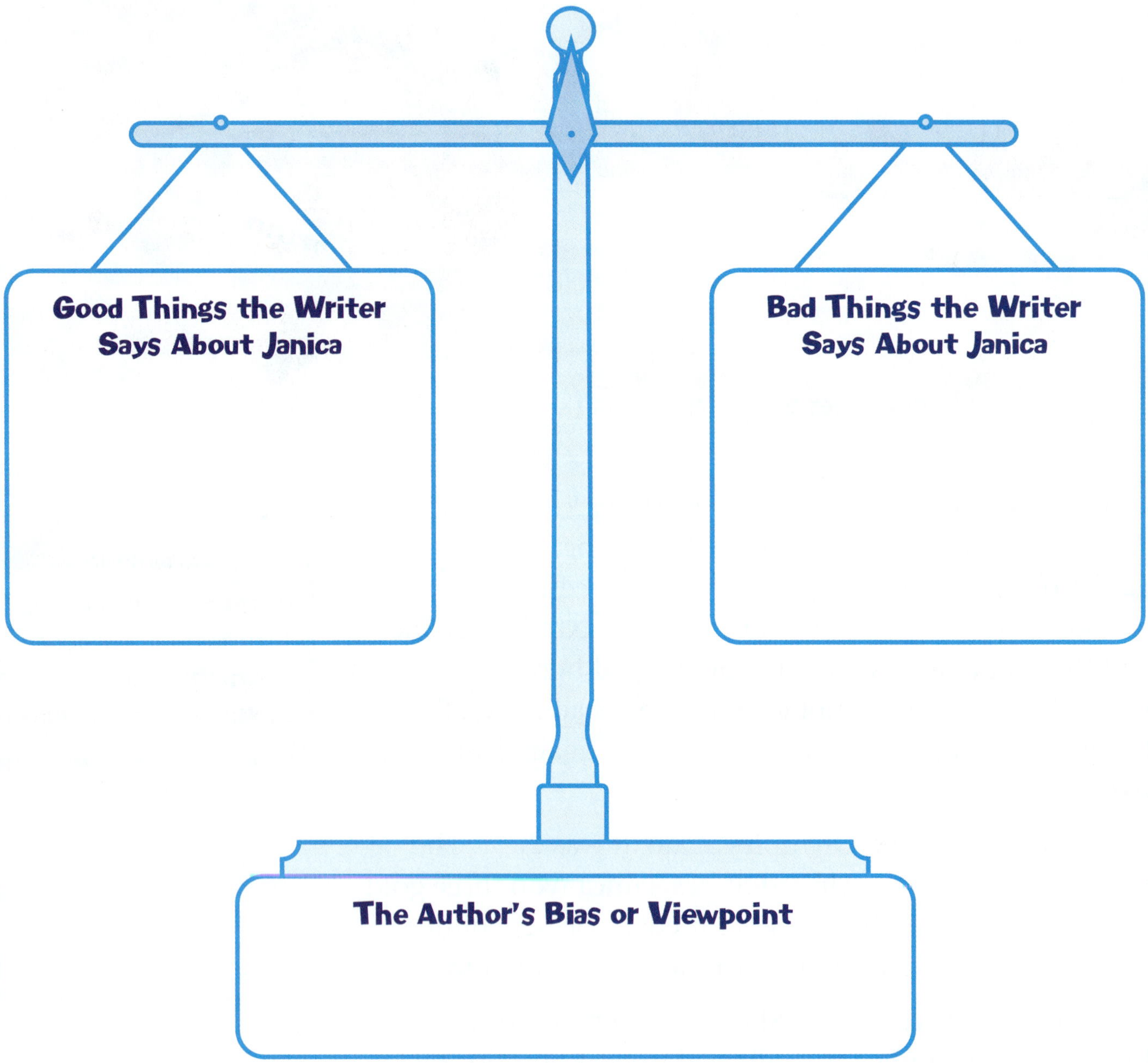

Your Choice

Circle the correct answer.

1. **What makes Janica a good skier?**

   A. lots of practice
   B. good skis
   C. weak knees
   D. a good coach

2. **Which sentence shows you how the writer feels about Janica?**

   A. At first Janica was not very good.
   B. Janica is a brave athlete.
   C. She fell all the time.
   D. Janica had three operations.

3. **The writer thinks that Janica is —**

   A. intelligent.
   B. fantastic.
   C. weak.
   D. dangerous.

4. **Which of the following is an example of someone who is determined?**

   A. a person who stops skateboarding after a fall.
   B. a person who avoids math because it looks hard.
   C. a person who gives up on piano after one lesson.
   D. a person who keeps studying even when the subject is difficult.

(See answers for Critical Thinking Skills, Lesson 6 to check your work.)

Number Correct:

Write Back...

Why is it important to know an author's viewpoint?

Lesson 7

Identifying an Author's Purpose

Your Turn

Read "Super Skier" again. Circle facts and information. Underline the writer's arguments. Highlight ideas the writer uses to make the writing fun. Then, add these to the graphic organizer. What is the author's purpose?

Inform	Persuade	Entertain
Facts or information used to explain	Arguments used to make you think something	Ideas that make the writing fun

Author's Purpose

Your Choice

Circle the correct answer.

1. **What was Janica's biggest problem?**

   A. She did not like to ski.
   B. She wanted to win medals.
   C. She did not speak English.
   D. She had hurt her knees badly.

2. **If a writer uses only facts in his or her writing, then he or she is probably writing to —**

   A. entertain.
   B. persuade.
   C. inform.
   D. describe.

3. **The author wrote "Super Skier" to —**

   A. persuade readers that Janica is a champ.
   B. inform readers about the rules of skiing.
   C. entertain readers with skiing stories.
   D. persuade readers to get knee operations.

4. **An invincible person —**

   A. always wins.
   B. takes risks only once.
   C. does dangerous sports.
   D. plays fairly.

(See answers for Critical Thinking Skills, Lesson 7 to check your work.)

Number Correct:

Write Back...

The next time you read something, how will you figure out the author's purpose? Why should you care?

BIGFOOT

Is it man, monkey, or myth?

Some people in Canada say they have seen a very large creature covered with hair. They call it Sasquatch. The name means "hairy giant." This creature has been seen in the United States, too. Here people call it Bigfoot.

For many years, people around the world have heard myths about these wild creatures that look a lot like humans. In 1811, a man even said he had found its footprints.

Is Bigfoot a **hoax**? Or could it be real? People have found strange tracks and hairs that are not like those from any known animal. Perhaps Bigfoot is an animal that science doesn't yet understand.

People who believe in Bigfoot say it hides in the woods and that it is **nocturnal**. They say it walks with long steps like those of a cross-country skier. It is said to be so strong

Comprehension Skills

You Have Already Learned

- Recognizing Facts and Opinions
- Assessing Evidence for Opinions
- Making Generalizations
- Connecting Across Texts
- Recognizing Bias and Viewpoint
- Identifying an Author's Purpose

People have reported seeing Bigfoot in wilderness parts of the United States and Canada.

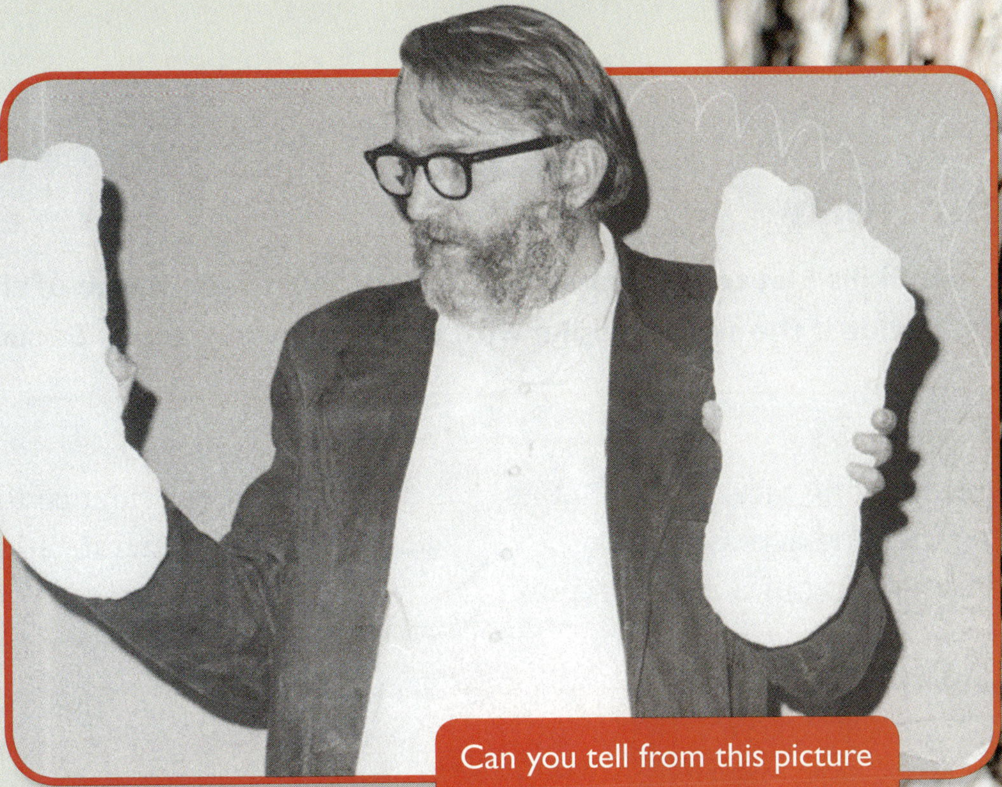

Can you tell from this picture how Bigfoot got its name?

that it can toss boulders and twist tree trunks. Sometimes it makes strange sounds, they say. It snarls and growls. It screams in a scary way.

Despite what some people say, most scientists don't believe that Bigfoot exists. No one has been able to produce any Bigfoot evidence. There are no Bigfoot bodies, bones, hunks of fur, or clear photographs. In 1967, some people shot some film of the creature. The image was blurry and far away. A famous movie director said that everyone in Hollywood had heard the rumor that it was a hoax. Now almost 40 years later, the only evidence of this giant creature is a footprint.

Is Bigfoot an ape, an ancient human, or a myth? People continue to argue. ■

Vocabulary

hoax: a trick
nocturnal: active at night

Lesson 8

Review

Your Turn

Use the Skills List to fill in the chart below. Write the name of the skill described. Then, decide if the skill is helpful with what you are reading. Explain why or why not.

Skills List

- recognizing facts and opinions
- connecting across texts
- recognizing bias and viewpoint
- assessing evidence for opinions
- making generalizations
- identifying an author's purpose

Skill	Is Using This Skill Helpful with This Passage?
When you think that an author is not being fair in his or her writing, you could be ________________	☐ Yes Why? ☐ No Why not?
When you can tell that a statement is true or just someone's idea, you could be ________________	☐ Yes Why? ☐ No Why not?
When you figure out why the author wrote a passage, you could be ________________	☐ Yes Why? ☐ No Why not?
When you come up with a broad statement about your reading, you could be ________________	☐ Yes Why? ☐ No Why not?

Your Choice

Circle the correct answer.

1 **Why do people think Bigfoot is strong?**

A. It leaves big footprints.
B. It can twist trees.
C. It takes long steps.
D. It makes strange sounds.

2 **The authors wrote this article to —**

A. share a story about an interesting myth.
B. let you know how large Bigfoot is.
C. warn you that Bigfoot is dangerous.
D. get you to believe in Bigfoot.

3 **Why might it be useful to read two different articles about Bigfoot?**

A. to see if the writers have the same information
B. to prepare yourself for a dangerous monster
C. to figure out how to find Bigfoot
D. to keep yourself busy

4 **Which of the following would a nocturnal animal like?**

A. people
B. skiing
C. darkness
D. daylight

(See answers for Critical Thinking Skills, Lesson 8 to check your work.)

Number Correct:

Write Back...

How can recognizing facts and opinions help you when you read?

Anansi and the Moss-Covered STONE

Anansi is pulling off a great trick—until he meets Panther.

Comprehension Skills

- **Lesson 9:** Analyzing Character Traits
- **Lesson 10:** Analyzing Conflict and Resolution

Reading Strategy

Stop and Think About What You Have Read

As you read, stop and think about your reading. Circle words that describe the characters. Draw pictures beside paragraphs.

Anansi the spider walked through the jungle. He was thinking about how hungry he was, but he did not want to gather food himself. Then he saw an interesting moss-covered stone. "What an interesting **moss**-covered stone," Anansi said aloud. Plop! Anansi fell to the ground **senseless**. When he woke up he shook his head, confused. He said aloud, "What happened to me? I was walking, I saw this interesting moss-covered stone and . . ." Plop! Anansi passed out again. When Anansi woke up he understood. You will pass out if you say "interesting moss-covered stone." Anansi smiled. He now knew how he could get some food and play a trick on his friends at the same time.

Anansi went to Lion's house. Lion had many yams on her porch. Anansi loved the sweet taste of yams. He was too lazy to gather his own, though.

"Lion, let's take a walk," Anansi said.

"That sounds lovely," Lion said.

What an interesting moss-covered stone.

Anansi learned to watch what he said around the moss-covered stone. Still, he wasn't prepared for Panther's trick.

After a while they came to the stone. Anansi said, "Wow!"

"Yes," Lion said. "What an interesting moss-covered stone!"

Plop! Lion fell down senseless. Anansi hurried back to Lion's porch and took her yams. When Lion awoke, she didn't know what happened.

Anansi did the same thing to two more friends. Giraffe lost his berries. Monkey lost his mangoes. Panther would not be so **gullible**. She watched each time Anansi tricked his friends, and she decided to play a trick on him.

She gathered bananas and put them on her porch. Then she waited for Anansi. Soon Anansi invited Panther for a walk. They came to the moss-covered stone. "Look at that!" Anansi said.

"What?" Panther asked.

"That." Anansi pointed at the stone.

"I don't see anything."

"Right there! See?"

"No, Anansi. What is it?"

"Don't you see that interesting moss-covered stone?" Anansi asked angrily. Plop!

When Anansi passed out, Panther hurried to tell the others about Anansi's trick. They each took back their food. Anansi was quite upset when he woke up. All the stolen food was gone. He did not learn his lesson, though. He sat thinking of his next trick. ■

Vocabulary

moss: green plant with small leaves and no flowers
senseless: passed out
gullible: easy to fool

Lesson

9 Analyzing Character Traits

Your Turn

Read "Anansi and the Moss-Covered Stone" again. Think about Anansi. Fill in information about what the character says, does, and thinks. Then, use the character's words and actions to decide on his character traits.

The character —

says

does

thinks

Anansi

Character Traits
How would you describe this character?

Clue
Use examples of what the character says, does, and thinks to decide on character traits.

Clue
Look at the character's relationships with other characters.

Your Choice

Circle the correct answer.

1. **What causes Anansi to pass out?**
   A. saying "interesting moss-covered stone"
   B. tricking Lion
   C. gathering yams, berries, and mangoes
   D. eating yams

2. **Which character trait best describes Anansi?**
   A. friendly
   B. brave
   C. selfish
   D. honest

3. **Which of Panther's traits help her out-smart Anansi?**
   A. She's honest.
   B. She's kind.
   C. She's clever.
   D. She's brave.

4. **Which characters in this story are gullible?**
   A. Monkey, Panther, and Lion
   B. Anansi, Panther, and Lion
   C. Giraffe, Anansi, and Panther
   D. Lion, Monkey, and Giraffe

(See answers for Critical Thinking Skills, Lesson 9 to check your work.)

Number Correct:

Write Back...

Which of Anansi's character traits are the most important in this story? Why?

Lesson 10

Analyzing Conflict and Resolution

Your Turn

Read "Anansi and the Moss-Covered Stone" again. What is the problem in the story? How is it solved?

Conflict (Problem)

Resolution (How the Problem Is Solved)

Your Choice

Circle the correct answer.

1. **What happens after Panther sees Anansi trick Monkey?**

   A. Anansi gives back the food.
   B. Panther uses Anansi's own trick on him.
   C. Lion gets mad at Anansi.
   D. Giraffe teams up with Anansi to trick Panther.

2. **What is the main conflict in this story?**

   A. Anansi keeps passing out.
   B. Lion loses her yams.
   C. Monkey loses his mangoes.
   D. Anansi is stealing from his friends.

3. **What is the story's resolution?**

   A. Anansi tricks all his friends and takes their food.
   B. Anansi gets away from Panther.
   C. Panther tricks Anansi and the animals take back their food.
   D. Anansi discovers why he passed out.

4. **What could cause you to fall down, senseless?**

   A. Hitting your head hard.
   B. Laughing really loud.
   C. Talking really fast.
   D. Thinking really long.

(See answer for Critical Thinking Skills, Lesson 10 to check your work.)

Number Correct:

Write Back...

What do you think of this story's resolution?

FLYING SOLO

Ruben sings like a pro when he's in the shower. Will he sound as good in front of a full stadium?

Comprehension Skills

- **Lesson 11:** Analyzing Mood
- **Lesson 12:** Drawing Conclusions

Reading Strategy

Make Connections

As you read, ask yourself "What does this remind me of in my life?" Your knowledge can help you understand what you are reading.

I can sing with my friends and I can sing in a chorus, but I don't sing **solo**. Mom is always trying to change my mind. "I heard you in the shower, Ruben. You sounded wonderful."

"Everyone sounds wonderful in the shower, Mom."

"Your father doesn't."

"That's true. Hey, I've got to get to the ballpark."

"I'll listen to you on the radio," she called after me.

I walked up the steps to the room at the top of the bleachers. Johnny and Miguel were supposed to meet me there to sing the national anthem. The announcer was getting ready to call the game on the radio. He turned to me. "Are you here to sing?"

"Yep. Me and a couple of buddies."

"Good. Hold tight, we've got a few minutes."

Ruben could not have guessed that singing in the shower would lead to this . . .

Ruben sings with friends. He sings in choruses. But he won't sing alone. Or will he?

I stood, shifting nervously. *Come on, guys. Don't do this to me.*

On the field the game was about to begin. The visiting team jogged in, and the teams huddled up. Then the coaches and the umpires met at home plate. The announcer flipped on his microphone.

I looked hopelessly into the crowd for Johnny and Miguel. *Please guys. Get here.*

"Everyone please rise for the singing of the national anthem." The announcer shoved the microphone in my face. "It's your show."

"I can't. Can you play a CD?"

"I don't have one. Go ahead, you'll be fine."

What could I do? I closed my eyes and sang. I sounded terrible, my voice almost breaking on the high notes. I've never been so **relieved** in my life as when I got to "*. . .and the home of the brave.*"

People **applauded**. "Hey, great job," the announcer said.

"Thanks," I said, and turned. Miguel and Johnny were staring at me from the top of the steps.

"Wow," Miguel said. "Way to go!"

"Yeah," Johnny said. "You sounded awesome, man!"

I shrugged. "No sweat. Just a **solo**." ■

Vocabulary

solo: alone; a song that a person sings alone
relieved: freed from worry
applauded: clapped loudly

Analyzing Mood

Your Turn

Read "Flying Solo" again. Fill in the boxes with examples from the story that tell where and when the story takes place and how the characters feel. Then, think about how you feel. This information will help you find the mood, or the feeling created by the story.

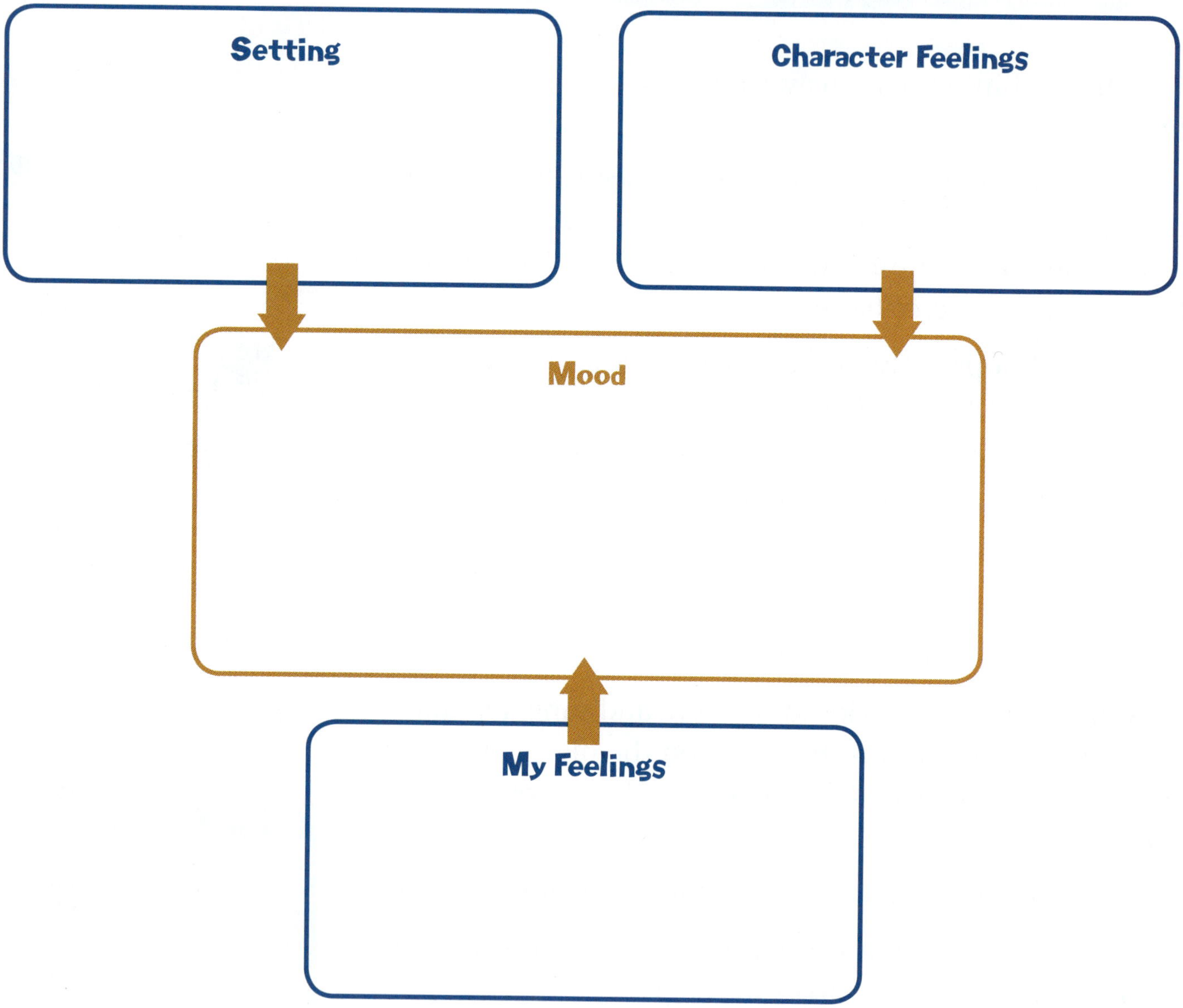

Your Choice

Circle the correct answer.

1 Ruben sang solo because —

A. he wanted to.
B. his mom liked it.
C. the guys were late.
D. it rained.

2 Which sentence helps readers feel what Ruben must have been feeling?

A. I can sing with my friends and I can sing in a chorus.
B. Miguel and Johnny were staring at me from the top of the steps.
C. The visiting team jogged in, and the teams huddled up.
D. I looked hopelessly into the crowd for Johnny and Miguel.

3 Which word best describes the mood at the end of this story?

A. quiet
B. funny
C. joyful
D. sad

4 Another word for solo is —

A. alone.
B. together.
C. pair.
D. again.

(See answers for Critical Thinking Skills, Lesson 11 to check your work.)

Number Correct:

Write Back...

How would this story change if Ruben didn't sing? Would that ending be better or worse?

Lesson

12 Drawing Conclusions

Your Turn

Read the clues from the story. Then, think about the story. From the clues, what can you conclude about how Ruben sang? Write your conclusion in the box.

Clue from the Story

I closed my eyes and sang, I sounded terrible, my voice almost breaking on the high notes.

Clue from the Story

People applauded. "Hey, great job," the announcer said.

Clue from the Story

"Wow," "Way to go!"
"You sounded awesome, man!"

Your Conclusion

Your Choice

Circle the correct answer.

1 How did Ruben describe his singing of the national anthem?

A. awesome
B. terrible
C. loud
D. wonderful

2 You can conclude that Ruben felt relieved because —

A. he had finished the song.
B. he realized no one was listening.
C. his friends showed up in time.
D. his microphone was off.

3 From everyone's reaction, you can conclude that —

A. Ruben's voice broke on the high notes.
B. Ruben sounded terrible.
C. Ruben sang very well.
D. The audience was trying to be nice.

4 A crowd would most likely applaud when they —

A. disagree with what they hear.
B. feel scared.
C. want silence.
D. like what they see or hear.

(See answers for Critical Thinking Skills, Lesson 12 to check your work.)

Number Correct:

Write Back...

Do you think Ruben would have been more willing to sing a solo in a different setting? Why or why not?

SPEED DEMON

Was the neighbor really a grouch?

Comprehension Skills

You Have Already Learned

- Analyzing Character Traits
- Analyzing Conflict and Resolution
- Analyzing Mood
- Drawing Conclusions

Speed Demon was the name of our go-cart. My sister and I built it last summer. We spread all the parts in the driveway, but we didn't know how to put them together. My sister **insisted** that the parts went together one way. I was sure they fit a different way. "You're wrong!" we shouted at each other. Within seconds Sara and I were too busy arguing to build a go-cart.

As we were arguing, Mr. Gonzalez stomped through the bushes between our yards. "Stop shouting!" he yelled. "I can hear you from inside my house."

Mr. Gonzalez was always yelling at us for making noise. We quickly gathered up our stuff and put it away.

The next day we got back to work. We sat **bewildered** as we looked at our wood, bolts, and tools. After a while Mr. Gonzalez opened his front door. "Oh no. It's Grumpy

Claudia and Sara didn't know how to put their go-cart together.

The go-cart was finally finished!

Gonzalez," I thought. Mr. Gonzalez took a look at all our parts and asked what we were up to. "We have to put this go-cart together for next week's competition," Sara explained.

Mr. Gonzalez worked with us for the next few afternoons. He helped us set up in our garage. He brought over some of his tools and safety goggles. Then, Mr. Gonzalez showed us how to cut boards with a saw. We sanded the go-cart. The smoother the wood was, the faster it would go. Then, we painted it red with big yellow flames.

On the day of the competition, Mr. Gonzalez put our go-cart on a trailer that attached to his car. All heads turned when Mr. Gonzalez pulled our go-cart into the park. We got a lot of compliments.

We didn't win the competition, but Mr. Gonzalez won first place in our hearts! ■

Vocabulary

insisted: said firmly
bewildered: confused

Lesson 13

Review

Your Turn

Use the Skills List to fill in the chart below. Then, decide if the skill is helpful with what you are reading. Explain why or why not.

Skills List

- drawing conclusions
- analyzing mood
- analyzing character traits
- analyzing conflict and resolution

Skill	Is Using This Skill Helpful with This Passage?
When you use clues in a story to form your own ideas, you could be ________	☐ Yes Why? ☐ No Why not?
When you think through how characters solve problems in a story, you could be ________	☐ Yes Why? ☐ No Why not?
When you figure out what kind of person a character is, you could be ________	☐ Yes Why? ☐ No Why not?
When you figure out how a story's setting makes you feel, you could be ________	☐ Yes Why? ☐ No Why not?

Your Choice

Circle the best answer.

1 **Which character is the hero in this story?**

A. Claudia
B. Sara
C. The go-cart
D. Mr. Gonzalez

2 **What can you conclude about Mr. Gonzalez?**

A. He was busy.
B. He didn't like kids.
C. He was a good mechanic.
D. He thought go-carts were dangerous.

3 **What was the author's purpose for writing this story?**

A. to inform people about how to build a go-cart
B. to inform people about go-cart contests
C. to persuade people that girls should build go-carts
D. to entertain readers by telling an interesting story

4 **"The girls felt bewildered." This sentence means they felt —**

A. crazy.
B. confused.
C. happy.
D. angry.

(See answers for Critical Thinking Skills, Lesson 13 to check your work.)

Number Correct:

Write Back...

Who is a hero to you? What are the character traits of your hero?

Brave New Friends

What makes someone brave?

Comprehension Skills

- **Lesson 14:** Interpreting Figurative Language
- **Lesson 15:** Identifying Genre

Reading Strategy

Picture in Your Mind
As you read, what pictures do you see in your mind?

Who Is That Masked Cat?

What's that you say?
You cannot come
For danger lives so near?
You need not fear
To go outside
For Wonder Cat is here!

As strong as steel,
With claws like knives,
He cannot lose a fight.
So come, you dogs
As big as tanks!
He'll beat you with his might!

This cat's a gift
To all who fear
Those hanging 'round at night.
For Wonder Cat
Is strong and brave.
He stands for truth and right.

For danger lives so near.

A hero can be big or small.

The Flea and the Dog

A flea, who was as small as the point of a pin, needed a home. "Where will I go?" Flea worried. "No one wants me."

Just then a **bedraggled** old dog walked by. Her hair was a dirty mop. Her ribs were ladders.

"What's the matter, Old Dog?" Flea asked.

"Who's talking?" cried Old Dog.

"It's just me," Flea said. "Do you want me to go away?"

"I do not care," said Old Dog. "For you see, I will soon die because I have not eaten."

"Why haven't you eaten," Flea asked.

"A young dog took my food. He eats his food (very quickly, I might add) and then takes mine. If I do not let him, he will hurt me for he is strong."

"Come with me!" Flea said.

Flea and Old Dog walked to Young Dog's home. He was chewing on a bone. Flea quickly hopped on his back. Young Dog scratched and rolled.

"Quick!" cried Flea. "Take your food."

When Flea joined Old Dog later, he lay down because he was tired. Old Dog asked where Flea would go.

"I do not know," said Flea.

"Stay with me," said Old Dog. "While you may be **minuscule**, you saved my life."

Lesson: *A hero can be big or small.* ■

Old, Old Stories We Love Today

A long, long time ago, a man named Aesop told stories. He used animals to teach lessons. These stories were called **fables**. Do you recognize these fables: "The Fox and the Grapes" "The Ant and the Grasshopper"?

Vocabulary

bedraggled: dirty; messy
minuscule: tiny

Lesson 14

Interpreting Figurative Language

Your Turn

Read each example of figurative language. Decide if each is a metaphor, simile, or personification. Then, write what you think the sentence means.

Figurative Language	Literal Meaning
Wonder Cat has claws like knives. ☐ metaphor ☐ simile ☐ personification	**The sentence means —**
The cat is as strong as steel. ☐ metaphor ☐ simile ☐ personification	**The sentence means —**
Old Dog's hair was a dirty mop. ☐ metaphor ☐ simile ☐ personification	**The sentence means —**
The dogs were as big as tanks. ☐ metaphor ☐ simile ☐ personification	**The sentence means —**

Your Choice

Circle the correct answer.

1. **What makes everyone afraid in "Who Is That Masked Cat"?**

   A. Wonder Cat
   B. fleas
   C. dogs
   D. knives

2. **"This cat's a gift" means that —**

   A. the cat came in a box with a bow.
   B. the cat is wonderful.
   C. someone gave the cat a gift.
   D. the cat gave gifts.

3. **Which words in "The Flea and the Dog" show how thin Old Dog is?**

   A. Her ribs were ladders.
   B. Her hair was a dirty mop.
   C. as small as the point of a pin
   D. for he is strong

4. **Which of the following is an example of Old Dog looking bedraggled?**

   A. She eats her food quickly.
   B. Her hair was a dirty mop.
   C. She was as small as the point of a pin.
   D. She was chewing on a bone.

(See answers for Critical Thinking Skills, Lesson 14 to check your work.)

Number Correct:

Write Back...

Describe a hero you know or have heard about. Use a simile or a metaphor in your description.

Lesson

15 Identifying Genre

Your Turn

"Who Is That Masked Cat?" and "The Flea and the Dog" are examples of two different genres. Use the flow chart below to find each genre.

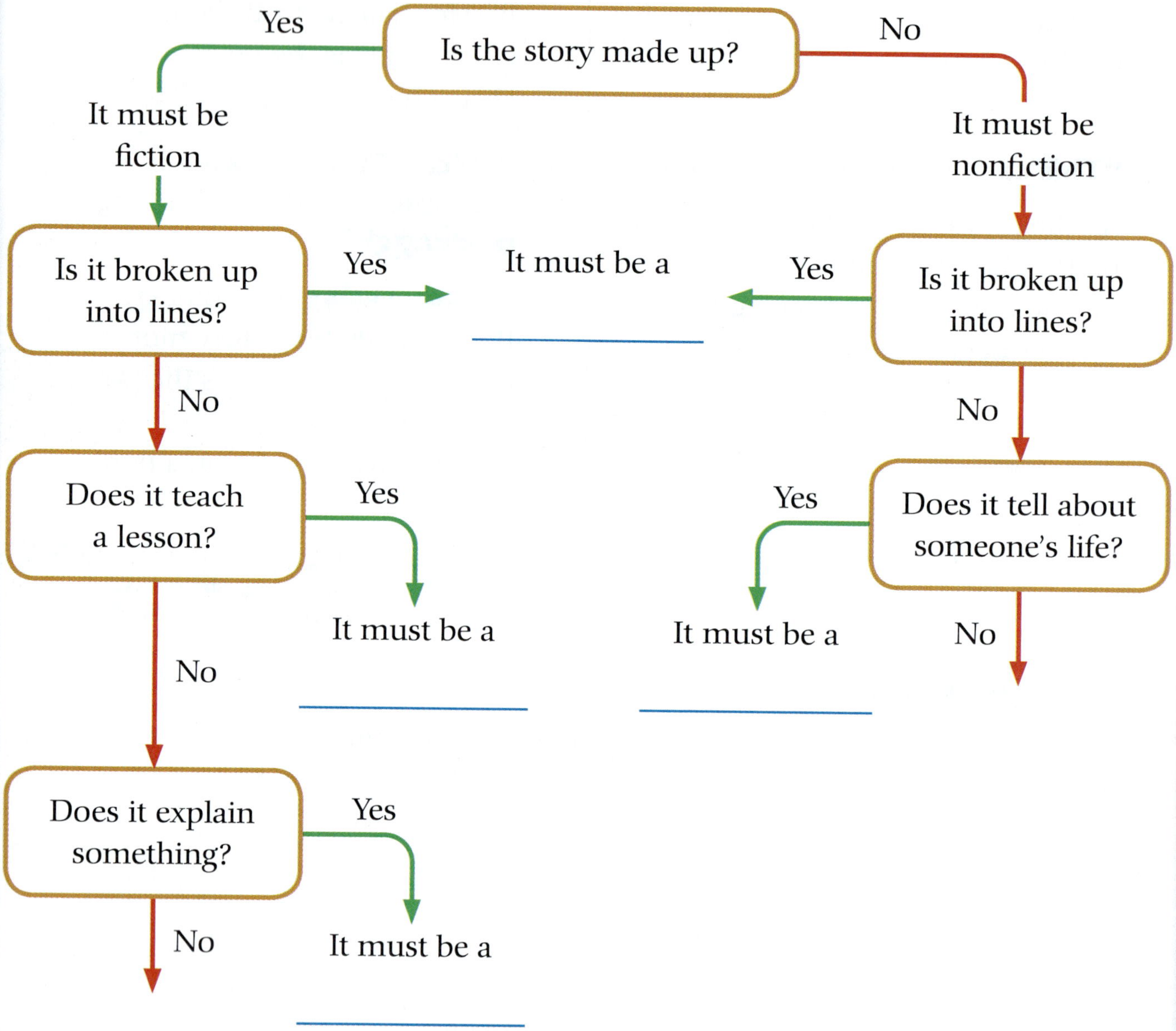

"Who Is That Masked Cat?" is a ________________.

"The Flea and the Dog" is a ________________.

Your Choice

Circle the correct answer.

1. **Why did Old Dog think she would soon die?**

   A. She felt sick.
   B. She had not eaten.
   C. She had fleas.
   D. A big dog was threatening her.

2. **You can figure out the genre of "Who Is That Masked Cat?" by —**

   A. looking at its format.
   B. proving the cat is real.
   C. counting its lines.
   D. reading its title.

3. **What is the lesson in "The Flea and the Dog"?**

   A. Don't eat other dog's food.
   B. Heroes can be big or small.
   C. Friends can be pests.
   D. Small creatures are lonely.

4. **When the dog says that the flea is minuscule, he means that the flea is —**

   A. kind and friendly.
   B. almost too small to see.
   C. his best friend.
   D. a brave warrior.

(See answers for Critical Thinking Skills, Lesson 15 to check your work.)

Number Correct:

Write Back...

Write briefly about a hero. It can be fiction, nonfiction, or poetry.

http://www.cantown.org

Can Town

How can you build a house with aluminum cans?

Comprehension Skills

- **Lesson 16:** Making Judgments
- **Lesson 17:** Summarizing

Reading Strategy

Use Background Knowledge

Many times, you already know something about what you read. Good readers combine what they know with new information.

In Lesotho, one of the poorest places in Africa, many people need homes. One young man found a rich supply of building materials in the garbage. The man realized that used cans could help people. The cans were made from steel and aluminum. Aluminum can **resist** water and can take hot and cold temperatures. The cans can be stacked easily. The man could even stand on top of an empty can and it would not **collapse**. He realized that cans were perfect building blocks.

Chairs, columns, and even gigantic candle holders can be made from cans.

Large buildings need a lot of cans.

First he punched holes through the sides of the cans. Local workers helped. They pulled metal wire through some cans to tie them into a row. These rows were stacked on top of each other. A board was placed on the inside of the wall. A few boards connected the walls and ceilings. A coat of paint kept the cans from rusting. Mud filled in any gaps. These houses cost little to build and the aluminum **reflects** the heat of the sun to keep the inside air cool in the summer and warm in winter.

The first house went up in 1996. These houses give people in Lesotho a place to call home. ■

Vocabulary

resist: to not allow a change

collapse: to fall or be crushed

reflects: changes the direction

Links | Recycle Anything | Can Fireplaces | How to Build a Can Wall

Lesson 16

Making Judgments

Your Turn

Read "Can Town" again. What did you think of the Web site article? Rate the article. Then, write the evidence that matches your rating.

How Do You Rate It?

Rating	Evidence (Why)
This Web site is really cool!	
It's a good place to check out if you're bored.	
It is a waste of Web space.	

Your Choice

Circle the correct answer.

1. **Why are can houses needed in Lesotho?**
   - A. Local workers can help.
   - B. Some people there don't have homes.
   - C. There are too many cans in Lesotho.
   - D. They have doors and windows.

2. **What two things are needed for making a judgment?**
   - A. character and setting
   - B. conflict and conclusion
   - C. opinions and reasons
   - D. genre and author's purpose

3. **Which of the following is a judgment?**
   - A. Some houses in Africa are made with used aluminum cans.
   - B. Cans stack together.
   - C. Can houses are an excellent way to recycle and provide shelter.
   - D. Aluminum reflects heat.

4. **If you cause a can to collapse, you —**
   - A. lift it.
   - B. crush it.
   - C. mold it.
   - D. fill it.

(See answers for Critical Thinking Skills, Lesson 16 to check your work.)

Number Correct:

Write Back...

What kind of writing would you make judgments about? Why?

Lesson 17

Summarizing

Your Turn

Read "Can Town" again. Then write information from each paragraph in the boxes below. Use the information in the boxes to write a summary of the passage.

Paragraph 1

This paragraph is about

The most important ideas are that

+

Paragraph 2

This paragraph is about

The most important ideas are that

+

Paragraph 3

This paragraph is about

The most important ideas are that

=

Summary

The passage is about:

Your Choice

Circle the correct answer.

1. **A can house reflects heat to —**

   A. Keep it hot in the summer.
   B. Make it attractive.
   C. Make it shine.
   D. Keep it cool in the summer.

2. **Which statement is the best summary of "Can Town"?**

   A. A man realized he could build houses from cans.
   B. The Web page is a hopeful one.
   C. Lesotho is one of the poorest places in Africa.
   D. Metal cans need a coat of paint.

3. **To write a summary you need to know —**

   A. how to support your opinions with evidence.
   B. how to make a good judgment.
   C. the important information in an article.
   D. the questions you would ask about an article.

4. **"Aluminum can resist water." This sentence means that aluminum —**

   A. does not allow a change in the weather.
   B. does not allow water to change it.
   C. does not allow water to change into ice.
   D. does not allow anything to touch it.

(See answers for Critical Thinking Skills, Lesson 17 to check your work.)

Number Correct:

Write Back...

Why is it good to summarize after you read?

COACH Pop

Meet the coach of a team that rules!

Critical Thinking Skills

You've Already Learned

- Recognizing Facts and Opinions
- Assessing Evidence for Opinions
- Making Generalizations
- Connecting Across Texts
- Recognizing Bias and Viewpoint
- Identifying an Author's Purpose
- Analyzing Character Traits
- Analyzing Conflict and Resolution
- Analyzing Mood
- Drawing Conclusions
- Interpreting Figurative Language
- Identifying Genre
- Making Judgments
- Summarizing

Basketball in the 1980s was all about the Lakers. In the 90s, it was the Bulls. Which team ruled at the beginning of the new century? The San Antonio Spurs. So what does it take to be the best in the **league**? Is it perfect shooting? Great defense? Or, did they have a secret weapon?

Yes, they did! The winning team had a great coach, Gregg Popovich. Or Pop, as he is known. Star players get all the glory. Meanwhile, Pop goes unnoticed out of the spotlight. Pop says he doesn't care if you know his name. For him, it's all about a winning team.

What's behind Pop's success? His game is all about defense. In 2005 his team had the lowest points per game (88 points) scored against them. If you can't score against a team, you can't beat them!

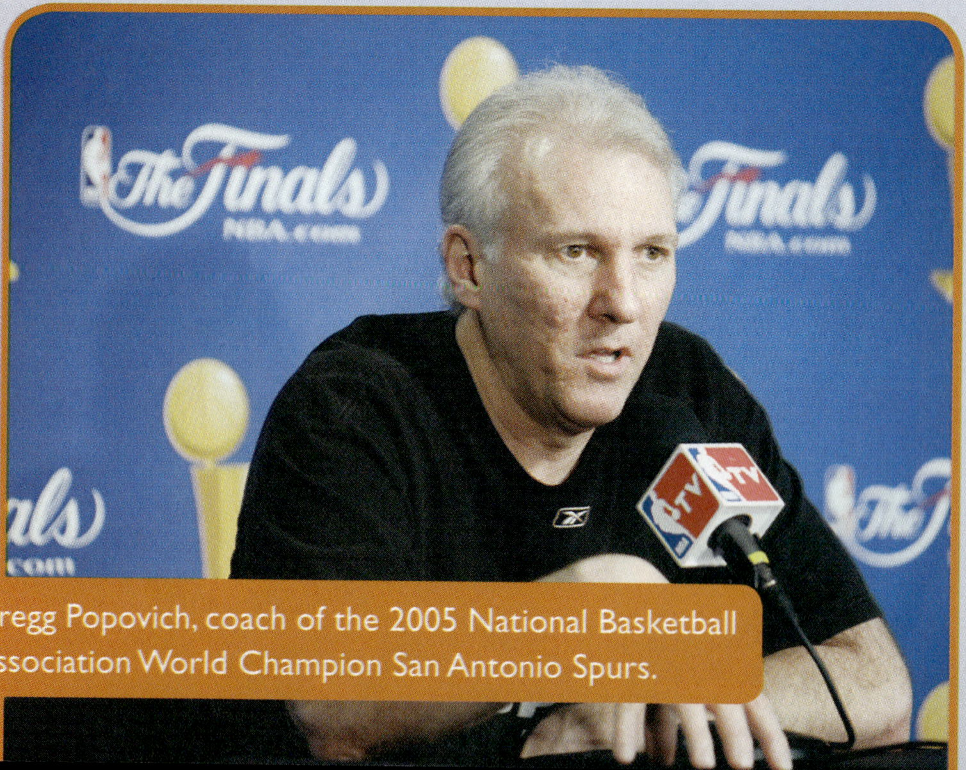

Gregg Popovich, coach of the 2005 National Basketball Association World Champion San Antonio Spurs.

Pop in action.

Pop also stresses **discipline**. Players who don't follow his orders lose their spot on the court. How does he keep a bunch of seven-foot millionaires in line? Pop says it's his military training. His years in the Air Force taught him about discipline. He has made some unpopular decisions. He kept a star player out of some **crucial** games. However, his team knows who's boss! They respect Popovich's decisions.

Why isn't Popovich as famous as some other coaches? Teams from larger cities like New York or Los Angeles get to be on TV most of the time. Teams from major cities are in the news, even when they're losing. Also, Popovich isn't in front of the cameras much. You won't see Pop doing TV commercials, as other coaches might. Still, a few more winning seasons should make Popovich a household name. ■

FUN FACTS

Pop's Winning Seasons

- 1999, 2003, and 2005 Championships
- 2003 Coach of the Year
- Assistant coach 2004 Olympic basketball team

Vocabulary

league: a group of teams that play against each other every season
discipline: training that shapes what a person acts like
crucial: very important

Lesson 18

Review

Your Turn

Use the Skills List to fill in the chart below. Then, decide if the skill is helpful with what you are reading. Explain why or why not.

Skills List

- recognizing facts and opinions
- assessing evidence for opinions
- making generalizations
- connecting across texts
- recognizing bias and viewpoint
- identifying an author's purpose
- analyzing character traits
- analyzing conflict and resolution
- analyzing mood
- drawing conclusions
- interpreting figurative language
- identifying genre
- making judgments
- summarizing

Skill	Is Using This Skill Helpful with This Passage?
When you figure out how an author uses language to mean something different from its literal meaning, you could be ________	☐ Yes Why? ☐ No Why not?
When you decide what you think about something you are reading, you could be ________	☐ Yes Why? ☐ No Why not?
When you retell the main ideas of something you have read, you could be ________	☐ Yes Why? ☐ No Why not?
When you tell some general things about the main idea and characters in a story, you could be ________	☐ Yes Why? ☐ No Why not?

Your Choice

Circle the correct answer.

1. **What does Coach Popovich believe in?**

   A. talent and discipline
   B. shooting and defense
   C. defense and discipline
   D. guesses and luck

2. **The author's purpose is to show that —**

   A. Gregg Popovich was in the military.
   B. Gregg Popovich is a winning coach.
   C. a star player was left out of some games.
   D. the Spurs should get more time on TV.

3. **This passage is —**

   A. a poem.
   B. an advertisement.
   C. a biography.
   D. fiction.

4. **A crucial game for the team is one that is —**

   A. difficult to sit and watch.
   B. longer than usual.
   C. boring.
   D. important.

(See answers for Critical Thinking Skills, Lesson 18 to check your work.)

Number Correct:

Write Back...

What critical thinking skills would you use for this type of career?

Independent Reading Record

Use the graphic organizers from pages 63–79 to practice these Critical Thinking skills with the other books you read.

Skill	Title of Book and Pages
Recognizing Facts and Opinions	
Assessing Evidence for Opinions	
Making Generalizations	
Connecting Across Texts	
Recognizing Bias and Viewpoint	
Identifying an Author's Purpose	
Analyzing Character Traits	
Analyzing Conflict and Resolution	
Analyzing Mood	
Drawing Conclusions	
Interpreting Figurative Language	
Identifying Genre	
Making Judgments	
Summarizing	
Review Critical Thinking Skills	

Lesson 2

Recognizing Facts and Opinions

Look for facts and opinions. Then, write them into the chart below.

Facts (statements you can prove)	Opinions (feelings and beliefs)

Lesson 3

Assessing Evidence for Opinions

Find an opinion stated by the writer. Write this opinion below in the top box. Write reasons the writer has this opinion in the next boxes. Then, fill in evidence from the passage that states facts supporting the opinion.

Opinion

Reasons		

Evidence		

Lesson 4

Making Generalizations

Look for related ideas to make a generalization.

Topic

Some examples say

Other examples say

Generalization

(A general idea that might be true in a lot of cases.)

Lesson

5

Connecting Across Texts

Write details that both texts share in the space shared by both boxes. Write details that are different into the boxes under each title.

Text #1 Title: ______________________________

Details Both Texts Share

Text #2 Title: ______________________________

Lesson 6

Recognizing Bias and Point of View

Think about the writer's feelings or opinions about the subject you are reading about. Fill in the graphic organizer below with the writer's words showing positive (good) and negative (bad) opinions about the subject. Sometimes you can tell the author's bias by which side of the graphic organizer has more evidence.

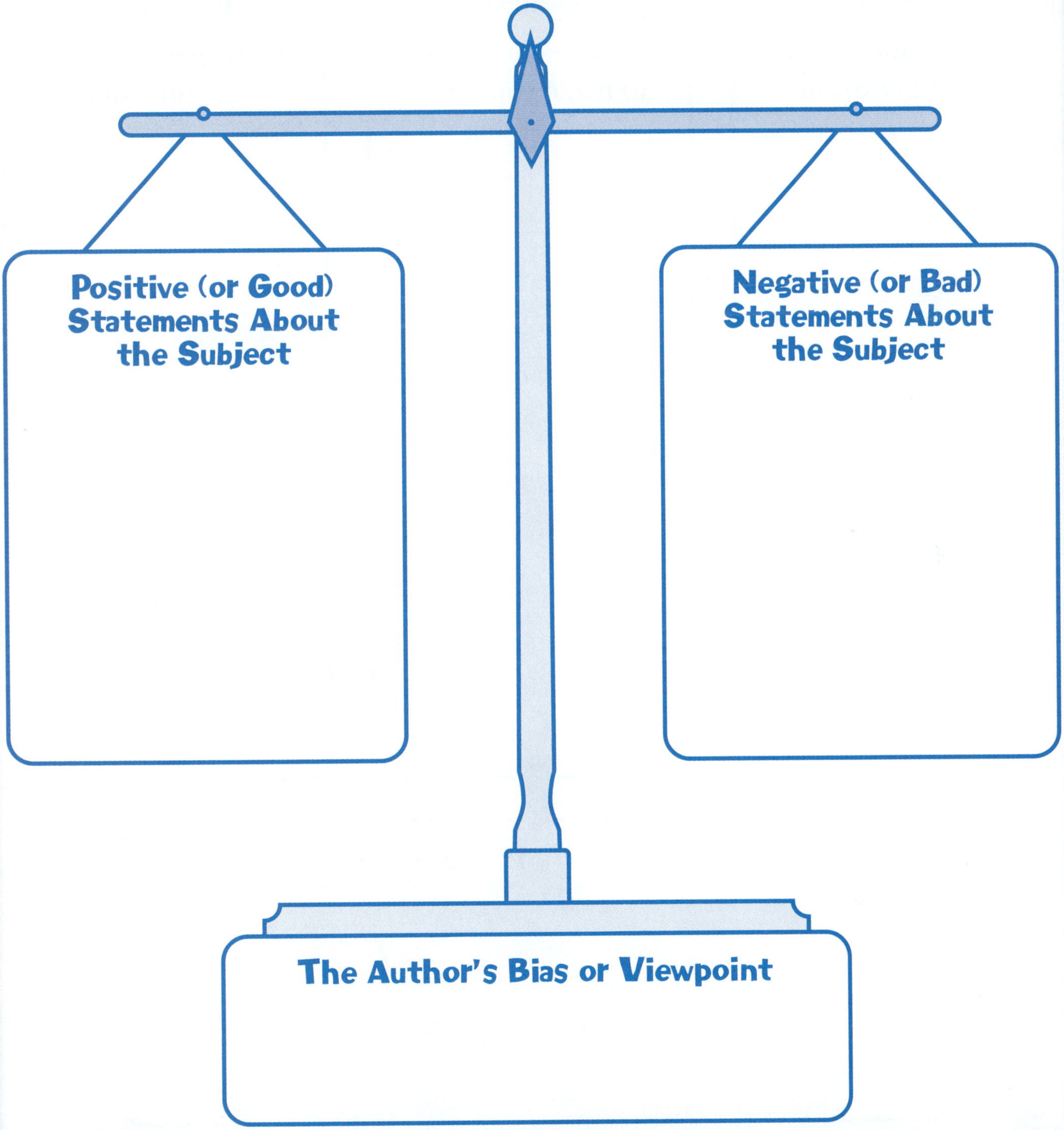

Lesson 7

Identifying an Author's Purpose

Authors have different purposes for writing. Look at the details the writer gives. Add them to the graphic organizer below. What do you think is the author's purpose?

Inform

Facts or information used to explain

Persuade

Arguments used to make you think something

Entertain

Ideas that make the writing fun

Author's Purpose

Lesson 8

Review

Use the Skills List to fill in the chart. Then, decide if the skill is helpful with what you are reading. Explain why or why not.

Skills List

- recognizing facts and opinions
- connecting across texts
- recognizing bias and viewpoint
- assessing evidence for opinions
- making generalizations
- identifying an author's purpose

Skill	Is Using This Skill Helpful with This Passage?
When you determine if a writer uses valid facts to support an opinion, you could be ______	☐ Yes Why? ☐ No Why not?
When you look for ideas that are alike or different, you could be ______	☐ Yes Why? ☐ No Why not?
When you see that an author is using loaded language to make a point, you could be ______	☐ Yes Why? ☐ No Why not?
When you develop a broad statement about your reading, you could be ______	☐ Yes Why? ☐ No Why not?
When you figure out why an author wrote a passage, you could be ______	☐ Yes Why? ☐ No Why not?
When you look for what can be proven and what is personal belief, you could be ______	☐ Yes Why? ☐ No Why not?

Lesson 9

Analyzing Character Traits

Choose an important character in a story. Then, use clues in the story to fill in the two boxes.

The character —

says

does

thinks

Clue
Use examples of what the character says, does, and thinks to decide on character traits.

Character Name: ______________

Character Traits
How would you describe this character?

Clue
Look at the character's relationships with other characters.

Lesson 10

Analyzing Conflict and Resolution

Fill in the top box with details about the problem in a story. Some characters have conflicts with other characters. Some struggle with nature. Others struggle with their own feelings or fears. How a character solves the problem is the resolution. Tell how the problem is solved in the bottom box.

Conflict (Problem)

Resolution (How the Problem Is Solved)

Lesson 11

Analyzing Mood

Fill in the boxes with examples from the story that tell you where and when the story takes place and how the characters feel. Then, think about how you feel. Fill in the Mood box with information about the mood, or feeling created by the story.

Setting

Character Feelings

Mood
(How the setting makes you feel)

My Feelings

Lesson 12

Drawing Conclusions

An author doesn't always tell readers everything in a story. Sometimes the reader has to figure out parts of a story.

Write clues from the story in the first three boxes. Then, write your conclusion based on those clues into the box on the right.

Clue from the Story	Your Conclusion
Clue from the Story	
Clue from the Story	

Lesson 13

Review

Use the Skills List to fill in the chart. Then, decide if the skill is helpful with what you are reading. Explain why or why not.

Skills List

- drawing conclusions
- analyzing mood
- analyzing a character's traits
- analyzing conflict and resolution

Skill	Is Using This Skill Helpful with This Passage?
When you think about problems and how characters solve those problems, you could be ______	☐ Yes Why? ☐ No Why not?
When you describe a character based on actions and words, you could be ______	☐ Yes Why? ☐ No Why not?
When you think about how a story's setting makes you feel, you could be ______	☐ Yes Why? ☐ No Why not?
When you use clues in a passage to make your own statement, you could be ______	☐ Yes Why? ☐ No Why not?

Lesson 14

Interpreting Figurative Language

Give examples of similes, metaphors, and personification. Then, describe their meaning.

Figurative Language	Examples	Meaning
simile a comparison using "LIKE" or "AS."		
metaphor a comparison that says one thing IS another.		
personification a comparison that makes a thing or animal seem human.		

Lesson 15

Identifying Genre

When you look for the genre of a piece of writing, use this flow chart. First determine if the writing is fiction or nonfiction. Then, figure out if it is a poem, a myth, a fable, or a biography.

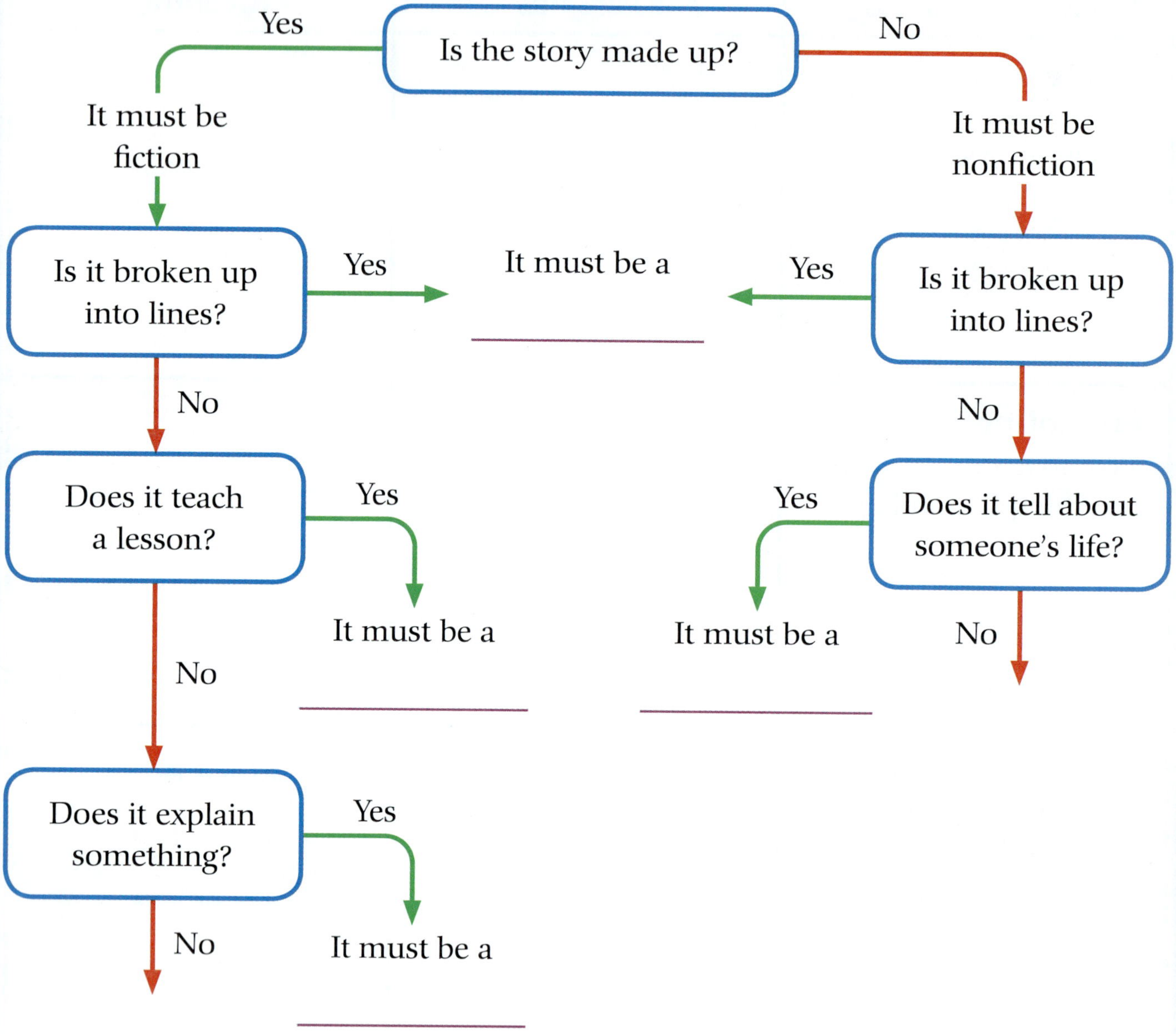

Lesson 16

Making Judgments

Put an X on the line to show your opinion of the article you are reading. Then, write the evidence that matches your rating.

How Do You Rate It?

Rating	Evidence (Why)
Excellent	
OK	
Terrible	

Lesson 17

Summarizing

Write information from each paragraph or section in the boxes below. Use the information in the boxes to write a summary of the article. Add more boxes if you need them.

Paragraph or Section 1

This section is about

The most important ideas are that

+

Paragraph or Section 2

This section is about

The most important ideas are that

+

Paragraph or Section 3

This section is about

The most important ideas are that

=

Summary

The article is about

Review

Use the Skills List to fill in the chart. Then, decide if the skill is helpful with what you are reading. Explain why or why not.

Skills List

- recognizing facts and opinions
- assessing evidence for opinions
- making generalizations
- connecting across texts
- recognizing bias and viewpoint
- identifying an author's purpose
- analyzing character traits
- analyzing conflict and resolution
- analyzing mood
- drawing conclusions
- interpreting figurative language
- identifying genre
- making judgments
- summarizing

Skill	Is Using This Skill Helpful with This Passage?	
When you figure out how an author uses language to mean something different from its literal meaning, you could be ________	☐ Yes Why?	☐ No Why not?
When you tell what kind of literature something is, you could be ________	☐ Yes Why?	☐ No Why not?
When you decide what you think about something you are reading, you could be ________	☐ Yes Why?	☐ No Why not?
When you retell the main points of something you have read, you could be ________	☐ Yes Why?	☐ No Why not?